10 THINGS

GOD EXPECTS

FROM YOU

GIDEON OJO

This Book

is a

Special Gift

From

____

To

____

Date

____

OTHER BOOKS
BY THE SAME AUTHOR

THE CHAMPION IN YOU

FAITH CAPSULES

TOUCHED BY LOVE FOREVER

PRAYER CAPSULES

10 THINGS GOD EXPECTS FROM YOU

GIDEON O. OJO

ACKNOWLEDGEMENTS

One of the scriptures that I find profoundly encouraging all the time is by Apostle Paul in Philippians 4:13 – "I can do ALL THINGS through Christ who strengthens me."

Having said this, I will like to thank the Almighty God, who inspired and strengthened me to complete this book. My God and my Father, without you, I can do nothing. I appreciate you Lord for planting this book in my mind, with your spirit working in my heart and gently bringing it to fruition. I return all glory and honor unto you because you are my wisdom, knowledge, and understanding.

To my Pastors- Nathaniel & Jumoke Saingbe, here is the fruit of your prayers, teachings, and encouragement. I sincerely appreciate the integrity of your lives, the anointing upon you, and your dedication to God's kingdom.

To Mrs. Ronke Adesina and Olawale Abaire, I owe much of the credit for this book, for their writing assistance, constructive feedback, proofreading, and editing skills.

I will like to express my immense appreciation to Chikezie Gloria Iniobong, my personal assistant, both at home and abroad. Thanks for designing the cover page, formatting the inside pages and all the other assistants that I cannot recount. God bless you and your families.

To my brothers: Mr. Ranti Lajide, Bisola Ojo and Larry Ojo who encouraged and assisted me at various stages. I say thank you.

To all those, whose names I have not mentioned, but contributed to this book at one time or the other, I say thank you.

To my faithful wife, Abiola, who kept me going all the time, thank you for your encouragement and support to pursue my dream with dogged determination. Your sacrifice of love, hard work, and patience are treasured gifts to me. We have come a long way, but I will never forget where we began.

To my children – The WATOB, the Lord keep you. I am proud of you and what God has been doing in your lives. I appreciate the love and support we receive from you all the time.

Dedication

I thank Christ Jesus our Lord
who has given me strength,
that he considered me trustworthy,
appointing me to his service.
1 Timothy 1:12 (NIV)

To every reader whose life will be
transformed
To have better and good relationship in
walking with GOD

Contents

Introduction

After what God did for humanity at creation; when he gave man His Spirit and a pleasant atmosphere to live in, does He still expect something from humanity in return? Will God give you a thing and expect something else in exchange? If He does, what do you think you can give to God that commensurate with what God did for you? What does God expect from you? Well, before you answer any of these questions, let me first show you what the Bible has to say about our God;

> **"For God so loved the world that he gave his only begotten Son, that whosoever believeth in him should not perish, but have everlasting life." John 3:16**

Nobody compelled God, or persuaded Him, to give what He had. It was out of His eternal decision that He gave Jesus to the world. And it cost God much to give His only begotten son. God gave up Jesus as the best sacrifice he could offer to reconcile humanity back to Himself. The sacrifice of Jesus' blood was a high price God was willing and ready to pay for humanity so that by his blood, the whole world would be saved from sin.

Consequently, everything worthwhile comes with a price. Whatever value you are enjoying today, someone somewhere paid the price for it. Therefore, there is nothing free; indeed, someone, somewhere paid for it. Nevertheless, you have a responsibility to sustain what you have received, and to treasure it so much that you do not lose it to negligence or not being dutiful. God had given unto us all things that pertain to life and godliness.

Consequently, He had enriched us with all the goodness of life, so that we do not lack anything good in life. There is nothing man will ever need to live right that God has not made available, in fulness, through Christ Jesus. Everything we enjoy from God today is by grace- the unmerited favor of God, through the gift of His son Jesus Christ. Jesus is the gift of God to us, through whom we have access to all that God had made available to us.

Our access to God is freely by the grace of our Lord Jesus Christ, who mediates between man and God. But, how do you reciprocate such a beautiful gesture to a God who does not require your money, cars, and all the material possessions you have? How would you show God you value the sacrifice of His only begotten son, even when He does not require from you your son or daughter? How much do you think you can give to a God who had done so much for you? Well, nothing humanly available can be given in exchange for what God had done. There is no limit to what mankind can give back to God in response to His sacrifice and great love.

God's requirement from you is neither grievous nor hard. Whatever God seeks from you is what you can offer Him. What He seeks to receive from you is what He has given you. You have nothing in yourself to offer Him that is not of Him. When God requires a thing of man, it is a calling- a calling unto a more profound knowledge of Himself. Being able to provide what God expects from you brings you closer to him. It is just a sense of responsibility that you value what He offers, and that you are ready to keep every instruction He gives to sustain what you have received of Him. God will never ask for your money because He does not need it.

God will not ask you to give him your food because he does not eat it, and He will not ask you for a house because He does not need a place to live. God's requirements are a heart that pleases Him, a heart that loves and obeys Him, and does every of His will.

Do you desire to know what those things God require from you are? Do you wish to know how to give them to God? Find out more in this book, Ten Things God Expects From You.

PREFACE

There is what to do for what to get from God!

> *"He has shown you, O man, what is good; and what does the Lord require of you but to do justly, to love mercy, and to walk humbly with your God?"*
> *- Micah 6:8*

Is it possible, that the God of the whole earth still expect anything from mere humankind? Could it be that there is a definite purpose why humans are different from all other creatures? What could be the expectations of God from us as humans?

Of course, there are certain things God expects from us as His most precious creature, made in His image and after His likeness. For everything we require from God, there is always something to do. There is a price for every rise in life. Even things that seem free are not actually free as such. Everything in life, when you take a closer look, has a price tag on it. Salvation is free but you must believe in your heart and confess with your mouth before you can be saved. Romans 10:9-10 says;

> *that if thou shall confess with thy mouth the Lord Jesus, and shall believe in thine heart that God hath raised him from the dead, thou shall be saved. For with the heart man believeth unto righteousness; and with the mouth confession is made unto salvation.*

The Bible says;

> *"But the hour has come, and now is, when the true worshippers shall worship the Father in spirit and truth: for the Father seeks such to worship him." John 4:23*

Awesome! Among the many other beautiful things God expects from us, worship seems to be an essential requirements that we must always do, as an expression of our gratitude, adoration, and praises to the Almighty God.

Interestingly, everything God expects from us is with just a singular aim- to bring us into a relationship with Him, where we will not only see Him as the Almighty God, but also as a father who loves and cares for us.

Truthfully, every relationship that will thrive must be mutual. Likewise, God desires a father-to-child relationship between you and Him. Nevertheless, this type of relationship requires a deeper level of mutuality, whereby you meet the terms and conditions that will foster intimacy.

God had done so much for you than you can ever imagine. He sacrificed much more than we can ever deserve. However, all He did was for you, so that you can come closer to Him and relate with Him, not as a slave, but as a son.

In this book, Ten Things God Expects From You, I will show you ten accurate expectations of God from all humanity, and how you can fulfill these expectations, which will improve your life and make you enjoy a working relationship with God as your father.

It is going to be a life-transforming experience, as this book will unveil to you some deep secrets of intimacy and fellowship with God.

And thou shalt love the Lord thy God with all thy heart, and with all thy soul, and with all thy mind, and with all thy strength: this is the first commandment.
Mark 12:30

Chapter 1

FELLOWSHIP

Have you ever talked to someone, and feel so glad and fulfilled at the end of the conversation? What about a person who listens to you always and never gets tired of your many words? Of course, you might have one or two persons like that; who you always desire to spend time with, simply because of the manner of the person's conversations, which is always filled with hope, life, encouragement, and comfort.

Now consider this: if communication with a fellow human could produce such a great effect of satisfaction, how much more when you commune with God in fellowship?.

What is Fellowship with God?

'Fellowship with God' means communion with God. It is a word with the Greek origin *'Koinonia',* which means an interactive relationship between God and anyone who has the new life of Christ. Fellowship is a thing of love- a thing of the heart. What matters most in fellowship is the state of the person's heart in fellowship with God, and not just some words or gesture.

You meet with God first in the secret place of your heart, and then, you gain access to His presence because God said;

> **The Lord is near to those who have a broken heart, and saves such as have a contrite spirit.** *Psalm 34:18*

Fellowship with God is an intimate relationship with your maker! The way a man goes intimate with his wife is the way God goes intimate with man in fellowship. This, in its real sense, talks about intercourse! Fellowship with God is a deeper sense of communion with the Almighty. In fellowship, what God sees first is your heart, and that is the state of your human spirit. God checks to know if you have come to Him with sincerity of a true and broken spirit, or just to fulfill some ceremonial rite. The truth of the matter is that your heart reveals your motive, attitude, and your real self; and this is why it is difficult for any person to hide from God, because the spirit of a man is the lamp of the Lord, searching all the inner depths of his heart (Proverbs 20:27).

True fellowship with God is revealed in an intimate understanding of God's divine nature and character. In such intimacy, you discover His pleasures and grief; you understand His feelings and feel His personality. Fellowship with God is more than "quiet time" or soberness. It is an active engagement with God in the spirit of faith, love, adoration, openness, and worship, which may, or may not, be quiet.

Until you come face to face with God's presence, you might not understand what He requires of you. The fellowship is the state of communion with God, where you will find out what and how much He has given to you and given up for you, and how much you can offer to Him in response to His love.

What God expects in fellowship is that you come to Him open-hearted, not mincing words or pretending to be who you are not. God expects your sincerity when you go to Him in fellowship. You show your level of openness to

Him by making known to him everything that concerns you- both the good and the evil. One of the beautiful characters of God is that he receives men as they are, and through communion, makes them what He intends them to be. Below are some of the ways by which you can engage in effective fellowship with God;

- **PRAISE HIM**

  > *Let the people praise thee, O God; let all the people praise thee. Then shall the earth yield her increase; and God, even our own God, shall bless us. God shall bless us; and all the ends of the earth shall fear him.* Psalm 67:5-7

God stated it categorically in his word; **Isaiah 43:21**,
  > *"This people have I formed for myself; they shall shew forth my praise."*

It is very clear and not ambiguous that God demands our praise and worship to recognize us and have a good relationship with Him. Praise and Worship is to give honor, homage, reverence, respect, to God. God demands worship because He and He alone is worthy of it. He is the only being that truly deserves worship and He is more keen to relate with those who praise, worship and adore Him all the time.

Praising God is a means of communing and fellowshipping with your creator. At every point in time, the Almighty God deserves our praise! Praising God is honoring Him. It is a way of appreciating God, and telling Him who He is, and what He means to you. Someone may pray amiss, but with praises to God, you cannot go wrong!

- **WORSHIP HIM**

> *God is a Spirit: and they that worship him must worship him in spirit and in truth. John 4:24*

God is seeking for true worshippers! That is, those who will worship Him in spirit and in truth. There are many today, who worship God with their mouths, but their hearts are far from Him.

No, these are not the kind of people God is looking out for. He desires those who will genuinely, from a pure heart, give Him unreserved and unpolluted worship. This is what true fellowship entails.

▪ STUDY AND MEDITATE ON GOD'S WORD

> ***In the beginning was the Word, and the Word was with God, and the Word was God. John 1:1***

Studying and meditating on God's word is another secured way of fellowshipping with God. As stated in the above Bible passage, the Word of God is God Himself! This simply means that you cannot separate God from His Word; neither can you separate the Word from God. In studying and meditating on the word of God, you gain access to fellowship with God. And as such, there will be definite and positive changes in your life and destiny. See what the Bible passages below say;

This book of the law shall not depart out of thy mouth; but thou shall meditate therein day and night, that thou mayest observe to do according to all that is written therein: for then thou shall make thy way prosperous, and then thou shall have good success. Joshua 1:8

But his delight is in the law of the LORD; and in his law doeth he meditate day and night. And he shall be like a tree planted by the rivers of water, that bringeth forth his fruit in his season; his leaf also shall not wither; and whatsoever he doeth shall prosper. Psalm 1:2-3

Studying and meditating on God's word is a sweet communion that results in a fruitful and blossoming relationship with the Almighty.

- ### PRAY TO GOD

> *And they continued steadfastly in the apostles' doctrine and fellowship, and in breaking of bread, and in prayers.* Acts 2: 42

> *Then shall ye call upon me, and ye shall go and pray unto me, and I will hearken unto you. And ye shall seek me, and find me, when ye shall search for me with all your heart.* Jeremiah 29:12-13

- ### FELLOWSHIP WITH OTHER BELIEVERS

> *Not forsaking the assembling of ourselves together, as the manner of some is; but exhorting one another and so much the more, as ye see the day approaching.* Hebrews 10:25

Fellowshipping with one another, as commanded in the above scripture, avails us the opportunity to fellowship with God. The word of God admonishes that we should fellowship together as believers in Christ Jesus. This is also because our coming together in fellowship attracts the presence of God into our midst and our lives.

Matthew 18:20 says;

> ***For where two or three are gathered together in my name, there am I in the midst of them.***

THINGS TO DO:

Ask yourself:
- How many fellowships do I have with God?
- Do I praise and worship God enough?
- How can I do better than how I am doing now in my walk with God?

Action:
Praise God and worship the Most High for His reigns and all His faithfulness and blessings upon you and your household.

Chapter *2*

HOLINESS AND CONSECRATION

But as He who called you is holy,   you also be holy in all your conduct . *1 Peter 1:15*

Furthermore,   then   we   beseech   you, brethren, and exhort you by the Lord Jesus, that as ye have received of us how ye ought to walk and to please God, so ye would abound more and more. For ye know what

commandments we gave you by the Lord Jesus. For this is the will of God, even your sanctification, that ye should abstain from fornication; That every one of you should know how to possess his vessel in sanctification and honour. 1 Thess. 4:1-4

Jesus Christ revealed the call to refrain from sin to his disciples, He said; *"Be ye therefore perfect, even as your Father which is in heaven is perfect"*. God is holy and perfect and He want does that will relate with him to be holy. He wants anyone that will walk with him to refrain from sin, grow daily and work toward perfection.

In excess the perfection God is requesting is separation and cleansing from sin and all defilements. God cannot have a relationship with anyone who has a sinful nature. **Amos 3:3,**

> **"Can two walk together, except they be agreed?**

God expects complete total concentration and purity if you are to have a good relationship with Him. Forsaking your sin to walk with God in obedience will give you a newness of life. Like the case of Joshua who was called out of sin. Joshua responded promptly to the call, walks with God in obedience and was able to have a sense of direction to lead the Israelite to the Promised Land. You must resolved **Hebrews 12:14,**

> ***"Follow peace with all men,***
> ***and holiness, without which no***
> ***man shall see the Lord".***

God is holy and He expects those who will relate with Him to be holy. **Isaiah 59:1-2**, explains how sin can separate man from God-,

> ***"Behold, the Lord's hand is not shortened***
> ***that it cannot save; neither his ear heavy,***
> ***that it cannot hear: But your iniquities***
> ***have separated between you and your God,***
> ***and your sins have hid his face from you,***
> ***that he will not hear ".***

Everything that exists takes after its kind. A lion will never behave like a goat; neither will a pig take the form of a sheep. Each animal has the exact identity of its parents. Likewise, as a believer, you have the identity of

God; your Father. The same DNA running inside of God is the same running inside of you as His creature. God is holy, and as a child of God, you are righteous by birthright. The truth is, the concept of holiness is the nature of God, who is our Father, and it must be revealed in us too as His beloved.

Invariably, when a child of God does not live Holy, it shows that the individual has not yet found his or her identity in God. Hear what **1 John 5:18** says;

> *We know that whosoever is born of God sinneth not; but he that is begotten of God keepeth himself, and that wicked one toucheth him not.*

The bible also says;

> **"And that you put on the new man, which after God is created in righteousness and true holiness."**
> *Ephesians 4:24*

Holiness, by nature, is an act of God, but the responsibility of holiness is the act of man. **1 Thessalonians 4:4** says:

> ***That every one of you should know how to possess his vessel in sanctification and honour.***

The responsibility of holiness is an unconditional obedience to God and the sacrificial separation from the spirit of the world.

Again, the Bible says;

> **"Therefore if anyone cleanses himself from the latter, he will be a vessel for honor, sanctified and useful for the Master, prepared for every good work."** *2 Timothy 2:21*

Indeed, God will never find useful, any individual who never rises to the responsibility of being clean from worldly influence, even as a child of God. You are like a vessel before God, and He desires to pour out His Spirit into you in full measures.

However, the Scripture establishes that God cannot use an unholy vessel (2 Timothy 2:21 KJV). This means that God demands your responsibility to stay holy before He can find you presentable, acceptable, and useable.

God seeks a Holy body, where His Spirit can reside. Will you make yourself available today?

> ***I beseech you therefore, brethren, by the mercies of God, that ye present your bodies a living sacrifice, holy, acceptable unto God, which is your reasonable service. Romans 12:1***

THINGS TO DO:

Reflection:

- Examine your life and trace every wrongdoing that may separate you from God.
- Confess your sins to God and ask for forgiveness
- Determined not to go back into sin or worldly things that can separate you from walking with God

Prayer Points:
- *O Lord purge me of every iniquity that does not glorify your name*
- *Oh Lord, by the blood of your son Jesus Christ, forgive me all my sins that go against your word in Jesus name,*
- *My father and my Lord, let your mercy prevail over your judgment in my life*

Chapter 3

OBEDIENCE

"If you are willing and obedient, you shall eat the good of the land." *Isaiah 1:19*

> *And it shall come to pass, if thou shall hearken diligently unto the voice of the LORD thy God, to observe and to do all his commandments which I command thee this day, that the LORD thy God will set the on high above all nations*

of the earth. And all these blessings shall come on thee, and overtake thee, if thou shall hearken unto the voice of the LORD thy God. Deuteronomy 28:1-2

You see, every divine instruction obeyed will bring a man to his land of distinction in life. Obedience to divine instruction is what brings abundance to the life and destiny of man. **Job 36:11** says;

if they obey and serve him, they shall spend their days in prosperity and their years in pleasure.

Obedience in the right direction can terminate a man's long term troubles and predicaments. Mary, the mother of Jesus at the wedding at Cana, said to the disciples of Jesus, whatsoever He, (Jesus) says to you, ensure you do it; because in there lies the answers to your questions.

(Paraphrased).

> **His mother saith unto the servants,**
>
> **whatsoever he saith unto you, do it**
>
> *John 2:5*

In verses seven to ten of the same chapter two of Saint John's gospel, Jesus instructed them to fill the water pots with water and they obeyed, He, again, instructed them to draw from the pots and bear unto the governor of the feast and they yet obeyed. And what we saw happened in that passage of the Bible was the blessings of obedience to God's instructions.

Just the way every Father requires obedience from their children, so does God requires your absolute compliance as His Child. Your obedience to God is the willingness to follow God, both when it is convenient and when it is not.

For instance, Abraham, a man of God, had his Faith strengthened and established in obedience to God, despite all odds. Little wonder God declared Him righteous, a father of Faith, and blessed among all men that ever lived.

Indeed, the blessing of God comes upon the obedient. You cannot obey God and not enjoy the benefit that comes with obedience. Christ Jesus obeyed the Father by submitting to the will of the Father and today, the name Jesus Christ has been exalted above all other names, both in heaven and on earth (Hebrews 10:7).

Everything Jesus came to accomplish on earth was the exact thing God wanted Him to do. Similarly, if you desire to be in God's perfect will, then, God demands your absolute obedience.

However, obedience grows! Your past acts of obedience to God will determine his present demands from you.

Jesus could not go through his highest level of obedience to God on earth- his death on the cross- at age 12 because his obedience was still growing. Abraham could not have attempted to slay Isaac if he hadn't been obeying God before then. Grow in your obedience to God, and you will eat more of "the good of the land."

> **"…And having in a readiness to revenge all disobedience, when your obedience is fulfilled."** *2 Corinthians 10:6*

God detests partial obedience; He wants it absolute. How much are you ready to obey?

Another way to see obedience is faithfulness. A faithful man is a man who is obedient yesterday, today and forever. Faithfulness is consistent obedience to the orders of God, and compliance with the terms of your relationship with God—in spite of the cost it entails.

The Scripture is filled with several examples of men and women, who lived a life of utter obedience to God's will. There were men like Abraham, Joseph, Daniel, Shadrach, Meshach and Abednego, Samuel, and many others. These men obeyed God continually, regardless of their frailties and shortcomings, as mortal men; they trusted God, and therefore obeyed Him.

Faithfulness is a decision. Though it is a demand from God, yet, it is your choice and your responsibility. Joseph was a chief slave in the house of Potiphar, the Egyptian officer. He was in charge of the house. One day, He was alone with Potiphar's wife, and she demanded that he slept with her; but Joseph REFUSED (Genesis 39).

Joseph had been obeying the commandments of the God of Abraham, Isaac, and Jacob as delivered to him by Jacob. He had been taught to obey God and keep following Him no matter the circumstances and the pleasure disobedience could offer him. This he put into practice as usual, when the lustful woman held him firmly to have affairs with him. He could have given in, had he not been faithful in obedience. He refused, he decided not to sin, and he was helped by the Spirit of the Lord God to flee. He wouldn't excuse his disobedience today by his obedience yesterday.

He knew the demand to be faithful. He knew it would cost him to refuse the woman, but he was much more aware of the Lord's desire, and he chooses to give in to God and not to lust.

What would you have done? Would you have obeyed God even under such pressure? Would you prefer to face the cruel wrath of a leader, rather than the just judgment of God? You might as well be found in such a situation in your life. God's demand is faithfulness. Choose to be faithful, and consistent in obedience.

What about Jesus Christ? He was the only man who displayed the highest level of faithfulness to God on earth. He had every opportunity to abort his mission on earth, but because he was faithful, he endured in obedience, even unto death. The Bible, in Philippians 2:5-11, says that Jesus had an attitude of obeying God, no matter the circumstances and the cost. Verse 8 says, "and being found in fashion as a man, he humbled himself and became obedient unto death, even the death of the cross." Jesus died because of faithfulness in obeying God. But he had to make the decision to obey Him. He made his choice at a critical time in the Garden of Gethsemane, when he was faced with the horror of the death on the cross that awaited him. Who would not rethink it? However, he chose to obey.

Just as Joseph REFUSED to sleep with Potiphar's wife, regardless of the consequence, Jesus REFUSED to abort the horrible journey to Calvary. In Luke 22: 39-46, Jesus again displayed his high level of trust in, and obedience to, the Father's will.

> **"...Father, if you are willing, remove this cup from me: NEVERTHELESS, not my will, but yours, be done."** *Luke 22:42*

The word, *"Nevertheless"*, shows the critical point where Jesus chose to obey God, despite His pain and sorrow. There is always a point at which you will have to decide if you will obey God or not. It may be for a minute, an hour, a day or even a month; but you will have to choose either faithfulness or sin. There is always a decision to make.

Faithfulness is a continuous decision to obey God and do His will, whether it's convenient or not. You, not God, decide to be faithful. Why would you be faithful? Why not give up? Because God is forever faithful.

> **"As it is written, I have made you (Abraham) a father of many nations, before him whom he believed, even God, who quickens the dead, and calls those things which are not as though they were."**
> *Romans 4: 17*

Abraham could obey the instruction to offer Isaac as a sacrifice because he TRUSTED God's faithfulness to fulfill His promises to him. He knew the character and Integrity of God to keep His word. So he could rest on that understanding, even at such a painful moment in his life.

Abraham trusted God to raise Isaac up again from the dead, even if he eventually sacrificed him. His faithfulness was fueled by his trust in God's character. Would you trust God's integrity as much?

God promised that He would make you a successful businessman. But now, He demands that you close down your ventures and attend to his present instruction. You wonder how you would be a successful businessman if you have to do such a thing. But, if you will trust God enough to take you exactly where He promised, by any means and different routes, you will obey him and close down the ventures. That is faithfulness, in consistent obedience to God, and absolute trust in His integrity.

> **"God is not a man that He should tell or act a lie, neither the son of man, that He should feel repentance or compunction [for what He has promised]. Has He said, and shall He not do it? Or has He spoken and shall He not make it good?"**
> *Numbers 23:19*

Awesome! The Bible mentioned above was the understanding that Abraham, Joseph, and the man Jesus Christ had that made them choose to obey God under great pressures.

Moreover, you will receive help from the Spirit of God when you decide for the Lord. Your fears might be that you are not sure of what awaits you if you obey God. You have thought of the cost and how hard it will be to cope with faithfulness because it is actually more comfortable and pleasurable, and cheaper to disobey God. But, may I encourage you with this? You will receive help by the Holy Spirit of God, if you decide to obey God.

Did you think it was so easy for young and handsome Joseph? But, as soon as Joseph declared his allegiance to God, under sexual pressure, he was strengthened by the Lord to flee. And in Genesis 39: 19-21, the Bible reveals that God was yet with Joseph. Even in prison Joseph was favored.

What greater consequence of obedience could any man face than that which Jesus Christ faced? Yet, he was strengthened to face it, and he came out victorious. Jesus received help, so will you.

> **"And there appeared an Angel unto Him from heaven, strengthening Him."** *Luke 22:43*

However, until you decide for God, you will not know how strong you will be against that temptation. You will receive help by the Spirit, just decide for God; He has everything in control.

There is an excellent reward for faithfulness. Joseph eventually emerged as the prime minister in Egypt. Abraham eventually became the Father of many nations, and Isaac was spared. Jesus became the Lord in heaven, on earth, and over hell. He was given the greatest name and highest place in God's Kingdom. It pays to obey God in the end.

THINGS TO DO:

Remember:

- Obedience is doing what God commanded you to do regardless of the cost or consequences
- To love God is to obey Him
- The word of God is the voice of God
- You will receive blessings when you obey God
- God requires complete obedient
- To obey God is better than sacrifice

Prayer point:

God please endowed me with the spirit to always obey you

Chapter 4

LOVE GOD, LOVE OTHERS

But when the Pharisees had heard that he had put the Sadducees to silence, they were gathered together. Then one of them, which was a lawyer, asked him a question, tempting him, and saying, Master, which is the great commandment in the law? Jesus said unto him, Thou shall love the Lord thy God with all thy heart, and with all thy soul, and with all thy mind. This is the first and

great commandment. And the second is like unto it, Thou shall love thy neighbor as thyself. On these two commandments hang all the law and the prophets. *Matt. 22:34-40*

Our love for God is not actually because we want to love Him; but because He first loved us while we were totally lost in our world of sin. He used His only begotten Son as a sacrificial lamb to redeem mankind from eternal death and damnation. Hence, our love for God is necessitated by His love for us. It is because He loved us first that we are able to love Him in return.

"For God so loved the world that He gave His only begotten Son, that whoever believes in Him should not perish but have everlasting life." *John 3:16*

How would you imagine that God chooses to come in the likeness of the mankind He created, just to save humanity from their sin? It is unreasonable today, to man and to the angels, that God became a man to die and save man, yet He did, because He loved mankind beyond reasons. The love of God supersedes human comprehension.

The love of God is a banner in the spirit that is raised for mankind, against every force of the enemy. When you love God and express your love to others, you raise a banner on earth for God, against every force of the enemy. So, together in love, you conquer and subdue the powers of the enemy in the spiritual and the physical.

You see, God first loved you, such that when you were yet a sinner, Christ died for you (I John 4:19). However, how do you show God, who first loved you, that you love Him in return?

- ●● Be Obedient to Him- You reciprocate Gods love by being obedient to all of His commands and instructions, as written in the Holy Bible (I John 5:3).

•● Live a life of Sacrifice- Sacrifice is what God demonstrated to us when He GAVE Jesus, His only son, as a ransom for our sin. Indeed, that was a high price to pay, which no one else can or will ever pay. Therefore, your love for God is able to let go of anything God requests from you (Genesis 22:2).

•● Love others- Your sincere care and concern for other people's needs is indeed an act of love that God requires from you (I John 4:19-21).

> *We love him, because he first loved us.*
> *If a man say, I love God, and hateth his*
> *brother, he is a liar; for he that loveth not*
> *his brother whom he hath seen, how can*
> *he love God whom he hath not seen?*

God expects you to express love, and live your life daily in the consciousness of Him that loves you first, and also love others unequivocally.

The greatest commandments emphasizes by Jesus are to love the Lord and to others. *Matthew 22:36-40*

God expects us to love other just as He loves us. The Blueprint of God, according to His word, makes it cleared to engage in loving others and never have no ill will towards those around us. We are to go above and beyond to be kind to others and help them in their situations, within our power and ability. *John 15:12*

We are called to love our neighbor as ourselves. *Matthew 10;8*

But I say unto you, love your enemies, bless them that curse you, do good to them that hate you, and pray for them which despitefully use you, and persecute you. *Matthew 5:44.*

Jesus made it clear in the book of **Mark 12: 29-**31 when he replied a Scribe who ask to know, what is the first commandment. Jesus answered him,

> ***"The first of all the commandments is,***
> ***Hear, O Israel; The Lord our God is***
> ***one Lord: And thou shalt love the Lord***
> ***thy God with all thy heart, and with all***
> ***thy soul, and with all thy mind, and with***
> ***all thy strength: this is the first commandment.***
> ***And the second is like, namely this,***
> ***Thou shalt love thy neighbor as thyself.***
> ***There is none other commandment greater***
> ***than these"***

THINGS TO DO:

Action:
- Recite: John 3:16 many times (to remind you of God's love to you)
- Think of loving God and other people more
- Determined to practice the love of God day by day by expressing love to God, to yourself and to others

Prayer points:
- O Lord help me to show love to you and other people every day of my life
- Beginning from today, I will change my attitude as I eagerly purse to love you and others with the help of the Holy Spirit.

Chapter **5**

HAVE FAITH IN GOD

Let not your heart be troubled: ye believe in God, believe also in me. John 14:1

It is impossible to have faith in a person you do not believe in. Similarly, your belief in God inspires your faith in Him too. But, how can you find a God you do not know? Or how can you have faith in a God that you have never seen? To believe is to see with the eyes of your heart, which become unlimited in grasping the invisible. Faith is a supernatural force that connects humanity to divinity! Faith gives man a better platform to relate with the Almighty God. God cannot be reached when faith is missing in action.

> **But without faith it is impossible to please him: for he that cometh to God must believe that he is, and that he is a rewarded of them that diligently seek him. Hebrews 11:6**

Of course, God has revealed Himself to us through His word, that by our study and meditation on His word, we will find Him and know His ways.

The Bible says;

> **"So then faith comes by hearing, and hearing by the word of God."** *Romans 10:17*

You cannot fully understand and come into the full knowledge of God without His word. God's word is God revealed to you in 'prints'. Therefore, faith in God comes by continuous hearing of God's word.

> ***For unto us was the gospel preached, as well as unto them; but the word preached did not profit them, not being mixed with faith in them that heard it.*** *Hebrews 4:2*

Consider this; you entrust your life into the hands of the pilot of an airplane to take you to your destination; even when you do not get to see the pilot, you trust the pilot's expertise. How much more would God want you to trust and believe Him for every decision and choice you make? When we trust God for something, we are simply putting our faith in Him to bring that thing to a reality. Psalm 125: 1-2 says;

> ***they that trust in the LORD shall be as mount Zion, which cannot be removed, but abideth for ever. As the mountains are round about Jerusalem, so the LORD is round about his people from henceforth, even forever.***

Sometimes, we allow worries; fear, anxiety and doubt make us disbelieve the power of faith in God. Yet, God expects that when the challenges get fiercer, your faith should get stronger and not the other way around.

God's word is His tool of creation. Hebrews 11:3;

> **through faith, we understand that the worlds were framed by the word of God, so that things which are seen were not made of things which do appear.**

God creates the picture He has in mind by speaking to you. When you hear a word, your mind sees it immediately, even though it is not physical—that's imagination. God's word is God's way of making the invisible visible and believable in your heart. Romans 4:17 says:

> **As it is written, I have made thee a father of many nations, before him whom he believed, even God, who quickeneth the dead, and calleth those things which be not as though they were.**

If God has not spoken, you have nothing to hold on to. But the Bible has been preserved for us to have access to the mind of God, as touching everything in life. God has undoubtedly spoken everything about everything in this world. It is left for you to search them out and reason according to the mind of God. You stand to lose many things when you care less to search out the mind of God, as expressed in the pages of the Scriptures. John 5:39 says;

> **Search the scriptures; for in them ye think ye have eternal life: and they are they which testify of me.** *John 5:39*

Now, faith is in degrees. You grow from faith to faith, depending on how much trust you have in the infallibility of God and His word.

> **"For as the rain cometh down, and the snow from heaven, and returneth not thither, but watereth the earth, and maketh it bring forth and bud, that it may give seed to the sower and bread to the eater: so shall my WORD be that goeth forth out of my mouth: it shall not return unto me void, but it shall accomplish that which I please, and it shall prosper in the thing whereto I send it.** *Isaiah 55:10, 11*

Trust is faith, which is rooted in the nature and character of God. For instance, you trust that God will not lie, even if what He promised is not yet fulfilled. Jesus must have trusted the Father to send the Holy Ghost to raise him from the dead before He could dare to go to the grave. Meshach, Shedrach and Abednego must have trusted the very character of God to deliver the them, before they could dare to go into the fire. What about David when he approached Goliath with only a sling and five stones? These were high levels of faith. But before they could do that, they had trusted God's nature which couldn't change for any reason. **Malachi 3:6** says;

> *for I am the LORD, I change not; therefore, ye sons of Jacob are not consumed.*

Again, in **Titus 1:2,**

> *the word of God says: in the hope of eternal life, which God that cannot lie, promised before the world began.*

That is to say, God can never change! He is the unchanging changer.

You will lose your faith at difficult points in your life, if you don't trust God's character. To have faith is not an all-the-time means to receiving good things from God, or to have answers to problems. True faith is rooted in trust, not just in answers. It is rooted in God's faithfulness and not just in his promises. Job, in all his afflictions and difficulties, had this to say:

> ***Though he slay me, yet will I trust in him: but I will maintain mine own ways before him.*** *Job 13:15*

You come to know God's character when you examine how he has acted and revealed himself in the past. Many have proved God's faithfulness through trust, and they have shown us this through several pages of the Bible. You don't only trust God in good times, or only when things seem to be going well. The test of your trust in God is known in hard and difficult times. When situations and challenges stir you in the face, and even though there are other alternatives trying to get your attention, yet, you need to trust God and demonstrate your faith in Him,.

God's words are "God's highways." The words of men are earthly and lowly, and the words of the devil are tunnels that lead down to hell. But God's words are highways in the spirit where all things are made possible. When you soak your heart in the highways of God; that is, the word of God, you will fly with wings and live a life without limitations. The word of God is a builder of destinies and a giver of inheritance for the saints of God. See what the word says below:

> ***And now, brethren, I commend you to God, and to the word of his grace, which is able to build you up, and to give you an inheritance among all them which are sanctified.*** *Acts 20:32*

Submitting yourself to the word of God is submitting yourself to the leadership of the Almighty!

THINGS TO DO:

Confess:
Romans 10:2
*"So then faith cometh by hearing,
and hearing by the word of God".*

Hebrews 11:6
*"But without faith, it is impossible to please him:
for he that cometh to God must believe that he is
and that he is a rewarder of them that diligently seek
him."*

Prayer Points:
- My God and my Lord, strengthen my faith so that I will uphold you to the end.
- In Jesus Mighty Name, I received an unshaken faith

Chapter 6

HEART OF GRATITUDE (THANKSGIVING)

"Oh, give thanks to the Lord, for He is good! For His mercy endures forever." Psalms 107:1

Thanksgiving means the expression of gratitude to someone, especially for what the person had done for you. As a believer in Christ, your thanksgiving should be unto God always, because no man ever receives anything, except it is from God. John 3:27 says;

> **John answered and said, a man can receive nothing, except it be given from heaven**

Your thanksgiving is a way of showing appreciation to God Almighty, for what He has done for you, and also in anticipation of what He is yet to do for you. This implies that thanksgiving is not only for what you have, but also for want you want, in the assurance that God is able to do exceedingly more abundantly beyond all that you thank Him for. **Ephesians 3:20;**

> **Now unto him that is able to do exceeding abundantly above all that we ask or think, according to the power that worketh in us.**

No matter what, God expects you to be thankful.

-1 Thessalonians 5:18,

> **"In everything give thanks: for this is the will of God in Christ Jesus concerning you".**

Apostle Paul knew the meaning of given a heart of gratitude and thanksgiving to God even in the midst of great adversity.

Paul wrote in **Ephesians 5:19-20** -

> ***"Speaking to yourselves in psalms***
>
> ***and hymns and spiritual songs,***
>
> ***singing and making melody in your***
>
> ***heart to the Lord; Giving thanks***
>
> ***always for all things unto God***
>
> ***and the Father in the name of our***
>
> ***Lord Jesus Christ".***

God finds pleasure in our expression of thanks and gratitude to Him. The writer of Hebrews in chapter 12 verse 28 expressed,

> ***"Therefore, since we are receiving a***
>
> ***kingdom that cannot be shaken,***
>
> ***let us be thankful, and so worship***
>
> ***God acceptably with reverence and awe"***

No matter what, God expects you to be thankful.
-1 Thessalonians 5:18,

> *"In everything give thanks: for this is the will of God in Christ Jesus concerning you".*

Apostle Paul knew the meaning of given a heart of gratitude and thanksgiving to God even in the midst of great adversity. Paul wrote in **Ephesians 5:19-20 -**

> *"Speaking to yourselves in psalms and hymns and spiritual songs, singing and making melody in your heart to the Lord; Giving thanks always for all things unto God and the Father in the name of our Lord Jesus Christ".*

God finds pleasure in our expression of thanks and gratitude to Him. The writer of **Hebrews in chapter 12 verse 28** expressed,

> *"Therefore, since we are receiving a kingdom that cannot be shaken, let us be thankful, and so worship God acceptably with reverence and awe"*

We are all aware of the popular story of 10 Lepers that received healing from Jesus in **Luke 17:11-19 :**

> **And it came to pass, as he went to Jerusalem, that he passed through the midst of Samaria and Galilee. And as he entered into a certain village, there met him ten men that were lepers, which stood afar off: And they lifted up their voices, and said, Jesus, Master, have mercy on us. And when he saw them, he said unto them, Go shew yourselves unto the priests. And it came to pass, that, as they went, they were cleansed. And one of them, when he saw that he was healed, turned back, and with a loud voice glorified God, And fell down on his face at his feet, giving him thanks: and he was a Samaritan. And Jesus answering said, Were there not ten cleansed? but where are the nine? There are not found that returned to give glory to God, save this stranger. And he said unto him, Arise, go thy way: thy faith hath made thee whole.**

Truthfully, God expects your heart of gratitude always. He wants you to be grateful for what you have, and for the things you are yet to have. In fact, when you are thankful to God in situations where you ought not to be grateful, then God shows forth Himself mightily on your behalf. A great man once said, "If you want a strange act of God, give Him a strange praise." It is strange to thank God when every situation suggests otherwise. But it is a requirement for greatness in the things of God.

> **Let the people praise thee, O God; let all the people praise thee. Then shall the earth yield her increase; and God, even our God, shall bless us.**
> *Psalm 67:5-6*

Thanksgiving is not limited to words of appreciation. More to thanksgiving are songs of praise, worship, tears of joy, and dance, among others. A thoughtful heart is a grateful heart. A grateful heart will produce a fruitful and blossoming life.

Indeed, if you will praise God today and show your gratitude to Him, God will raise you above all limitations of life.

THINGS TO DO:

Ask yourself:

- Do I adequately grateful to God every day?
- How can I improve my appreciation to God for all His deeds in my life.

Prayer Points:

- O Lord I ask for mercy in all areas that I have come short of my gratitude to you.
- Please endow me with the spirit of gratitude henceforth

Chapter 7

WITNESS FOR HIM

"You did not choose me, but I chose you and appointed you that you should go and bear fruit, and that your fruit should remain, that whatever you ask the Father in My name He may give you." John 15:16

The last commanded Jesus gave his disciple before he departed is found in **Matthew 28:19-20,**

> *Go ye therefore, and teach all nations,*
> *baptizing them in the name of the Father,*
> *and of the Son, and of the Holy Ghost.*
> *Teaching them to observe all things*
> *whatsoever I have commanded you*
> *and, lo I am with you always, even unto*
> *the end of the world. Amen.*

God commanded it and expects us to tell others about Him and His power". Our witnessing to others is of utmost important to God and to us to expand the kingdom of God. Christ commanded us to tell others about Him and promised to give us the power to do. **Acts 1:8,**

> *"But ye shall receive power, after*
> *that the Holy Ghost is come upon you:*
> *and ye shall be witnesses unto me*
> *both in Jerusalem, and in all Judaea,*
> *and in Samaria, and unto the uttermost*
> *part of the earth.*

Romans 10:14, also explained why we need to evangelize for God,

> *"How then shall they call on him in*
> *whom they have not believed? and*
> *how shall they believe in him of*
> *whom they have not heard?*

and how shall they hear without a preacher? Therefore,

> ***"Go ye into all the world, and preach
> the gospel to every creature".*** Mark 16:15

It will interest you to know that God's heart cry is the soul of mankind. God desires that all men be saved (I Timothy 2:4). Therefore, as a believer in Christ, you have a responsibility to tell others about the saving grace of our Lord Jesus Christ. This is the concept about witnessing for God.

Witnessing for God also entails making disciples for God. Discipleship is God's command to every believer. **Matthew 28:19;**

> ***Go ye therefore, and teach all nations,***
>
> ***baptizing them in the name of the Father,***
>
> ***and the Son, and of the Holy Ghost:***
>
> ***Teaching them to observe all things***
>
> ***whatsoever I have commanded you:***
>
> ***and, lo, I am with you always, even unto***
>
> ***the end of the world.***

If you truly seek the Lord, you will invariably seek after the lost. Every word of God spoken to you is not to remain a secret, but after it had changed you, let it change others. The Bible was not kept a secret from us; otherwise we would be short of the knowledge of God. God redeemed our souls from destruction and condemnation, so that through our lives also, others can come to the saving knowledge and redemptive power of Christ.

More so, the reason God did not allow death to take you away at salvation is simply because He wants you to carry out the assignment of witnessing judiciously. God loves you and that was why he sent His son to save you. Therefore, He is at this time sending you also to tell others about the Love of our dear God and the saving grace of our Lord Jesus Christ. His utmost desire is not for any to perish, but that all should repent from their sins.

For God sent not his Son into the world to condemn the world; but that the world through him might be saved. He that believeth on him is not condemned: but he that believeth not is condemned already, because he hath not believed in the name of the only begotten Son of God. Jn 3:17-18

THINGS TO DO:

Affirmation:

- Henceforth, I will make it a point of duty to share the word of God anywhere, anytime
- I will not take it for granted to spread the gospel of Jesus Christ and His power

Prayer points:

- O Lord equipped and empowered me to witness for you as you have commanded.
- I receive the courage to evangelize wherever I find myself without shame

Chapter 8

FORGIVE

> *"And forgive us our debts as we forgive our debtors…. For if ye forgive men their trespasses, your heavenly Father will also forgive you: but if you forgive not men their trespasses, neither will God forgive thee."*
> *Matthew 6: 12, 14, 15*

Forgiveness is an essential aspect of human life, which allows you to live in the fullness of joy and happiness, and it strengthens peaceful coexistence with everyone around you.

Indeed, people will offend you. They will wrong you and despise you. Nevertheless, you must not allow grudges, hatred, and anger to find expression in your heart against people around you. These attitudes keep you from forgiving and they harden your heart against your neighbor.

But, God had demonstrated forgiveness first to us, in that, when we were yet sinners, Christ died for us **(Romans 5:8).**

> **But God commandeth his love towards us, in that, while we were yet sinners, Christ died for us.**

It will interest you to know that when God forgave you, He did it once and for all, through the blood of His dear Son, Jesus Christ. God forgave you of your sins and saved your soul from damnation forever (Hebrew 10:14). However, you must work out your salvation with fear and trembling!

Now, God expects you to show forgiveness to others because;

- Forgiveness is a command from God.

- God taught us forgiveness, using His life as an example.

- God could forgive you too.

- You need to forgive others to live in peace and happiness.

A life that forgives is a life that will live in good health. Unforgiveness is like cancer that eats its victim up day and night. Unforgiveness is poisonous and deadly. There is liberty in forgiving others, and greater freedom in forgiving oneself- anytime. There are many sicknesses rooted in bitterness and unforgiveness. They are referred to as psychosomatic sicknesses. They are rooted in the soul, which is also the seat of bitterness. No one can ever be bitter, and be better at the same time. Bitterness denies you the freedom of peace and joy. You will do yourself great harm by keeping offenses in your heart without forgiving men. When you are bitter against anyone, you become devoid of the spirit of joy, which is what gives you access to God's presence, and to the unlimited resources of heaven that are available to us upon redemption. Isaiah 12:3 says:

> ***Therefore with joy shall ye draw water from the wells of salvation.***

Again, it says in Philippians 4:4:

> ***Rejoice in the Lord always; and again I say, Rejoice.***

You must guide your heart to be void of bitterness. The spirit of joy cannot thrive where there is bitterness. Joy is your access code to God's presence and attention. If anything succeeds in tampering with your joy, that thing has succeeded in tampering with your life. When joy is absent in your heart, God will not be present; and this chain reaction ends up affecting every other thing around you. See what the scripture says about this below:

> **The vine is dried up, and the fig tree languisheth; the pomegranate tree, the palm tree also, and the apple trees, even all the trees of the field, are withered: because joy is withered away from the sons of men. Joel 1:12**

Asides the spiritual consequences, you also subject yourself to psychological and physiological diseases. Again, forgiveness releases you to live in freedom without any tension. You see men as fallible, just as you are, and you accept men as imperfect. You must give allowance for misunderstanding and offense, and be ready to forgive anyone who offends you. This is one of the secrets of a peaceful and healthy life. You live a life free of bitterness and frustration by forgiving men.

Most importantly, forgive yourself! The way God sees you when you don't forgive others, is the same way He sees you when you don't forgive yourself. When things go wrong because you caused them, you need to forgive yourself and not hold on to bitterness against yourself. It is even worse not to forgive yourself, than it is not to forgive others. If you sin against God and you confess it to God and ask for forgiveness, and He forgives you; forgive yourself too. If you offend another man and he eventually forgives you, forgive yourself also. If God has declared you forgiven, then in heaven and earth, you are forgiven. If a man has forgiven you your offense against him, then you are forgiven.

What have you held against others that you wouldn't give up? What have you held against yourself, as the reason for some failures? You need to release others and yourself in forgiveness. Will you give what God requires now? Go ahead right away, call that man, and that woman that you need to practically release from your heart, so that you can walk in the liberty you have through Christ. Yes! Free yourself now from that heavy burden and bitterness, as you free that man, and that woman, from your heart today. Praise God!

> **Stand fast therefore in the liberty wherewith Christ hath made us free, and be not entangled again with the yoke of bondage.** *Galatians 5:1*

THINGS TO DO:

Action:
As from today, I will make "Mark 11 verses 25" My daily reminder to remember that I must forgive others, so God will also forgive me
**"When ye stand praying, forgive,
if ye have ought against any:
that your Father also which is in heaven
may forgive you your trespasses".**

Action:
Think about all of the people who have offended you and plan to forgive them.

Prayer points:
- Oh Lord, forgive me today and set my heart free from all fears
- I received the heart of forgiveness today by the power of the Holy Spirit

Chapter 9

FRUITFULNESS

"Then God blessed them, and God said to them, "Be fruitful and multiply; fill the earth and subdue it; have dominion over the fish of the sea, over the birds of the air, and over every living thing that moves on the earth." *Genesis 1:28*

L et us consider this; God designed the tree to bear fruits and seeds, which are essential for the survival and posterity of the tree. So, a tree that does not bear fruit will soon lose its relevance, and go into extinction, even though that wasn't God's plan for the tree.

Similarly, God created you to be fruitful, multiply, and have dominion (Genesis 1:28). You are designed for abundance and increase. God created you for more and expected you to be fruitful. See what Jesus said about fruit bearing in the passage below:

> ***I am the true vine, and my Father is the husbandman. <u>Every branch in me that beareth not fruit he taketh away:</u> and every branch that beareth fruit, he purgeth it, that it may bring forth more fruit. John 15:1-2***

John 15:16,

> ***"Ye have not chosen me, but I have chosen you, and ordained you, that ye should go and bring forth fruit, and that your fruit should remain: that whatsoever ye shall ask of the Father in my name, he may give it to you".***

God expects you to be fruitful in your spirit, soul, and body. You see, as much as God desires fruitfulness for you in your spirit, He also wants you to prosper in your business, career, and family. Subsequently, once you become fruitful in all these aspects of life, it becomes easy for you to advance God's Kingdom on earth. The seed of God is in you, and it is expected to grow unto fruitfulness. Work out growth in every area of your life. When you discover God's gift in you, it is a seed; and you must grow it. You are responsible for the BEARING, but God is responsible for the SEEDING.

2 Corinthians 9:10 says,

> *Now he that ministereth seed to the sower, both minister bread for your food, and multiply your seed sown, and increase the fruits of your righteousness.*

For every increase God brings to you, there is a seed inside of it that must be sown, in order to bear more fruits to produce bread, and more seeds that must be sown back, to enable continuity.

God's expects that you make effective use of the resources He had made available to you. But, a question you will need to answer now, is, how fruitful are my with the resources God has committed into my hands? Are my truly diligent with the gifts, talents or resources He gave to me? The account of a man below, who before traveling to a far country, gave his servants talents according to their abilities, will give us a clear understanding of what, and how, God expects us to be fruitful with whatsoever is entrusted in our care.

> *For the kingdom of heaven is as a man travelling into a far country, who called his own servants, and delivered unto them his goods. And unto one he gave five talents, to another two, and to another one; to every man according to his several ability; and straightway took his journey. Then he that had received*

the five talents went and traded with the same, and made them other five talents. And likewise he that had received two, he also gained other two. But he that had received one went and digged in the earth, and hid his lord's money. After a long time, the lord of those servants cometh, and reckoneth with them. And so he that had received five talents came and brought other five talents, saying, Lord, thou deliveredst unto me five talents: behold, I have gained beside them five talents more. His lord said unto him, Well done, thou good and faithful servant: thou hast been faithful over a few things, I will make thee ruler over many things: enter thou into the joy of thy lord. He also that had received two talents came and said, Lord, thou deliveredst unto me two talents: behold, I have gained two other talents beside them. His lord said unto him, Well done, good and faithful servant; thou hast been faithful over a few things, I will make thee ruler over many things:

enter thou into the joy of thy lord. Then he which had received the one talent came and said, Lord, I knew thee that thou art an hard man, reaping where thou hast not sown, and gathering where thou hast not strawed: And I was afraid, and went and hid thy talent in the earth: lo, there thou hast that is thine. His lord answered and said unto him, Thou wicked and slothful servant, thou knewest that I reap where I sowed not, and gather where I have not strawed: Thou oughtest therefore to have put my money to the exchangers, and then at my coming I should have received mine own with usury. Take therefore the talent from him, and give it unto him which hath ten talents. For unto every one that hath shall be given, and he shall have abundance: but from him that hath not shall be taken away even that which he hath. And cast ye the unprofitable servant into outer darkness: there shall be weeping and gnashing of teeth. Matthew 25:14-30

THINGS TO DO:

Ask yourself:
- Do I make use of the gifts and talents God has given to me for His glory?
- God has created me to fulfill purpose - Am I fulfilling God's purpose?
- How better can I use God's potentials to better His glory and the world?

Prayer Points:
- I decree by the Power of the Holy Ghost for the power of fruitfulness to cause me
- Multiply and grow in all areas of my life and for God's glory
- Oh Lord, turn all my barrenness to fruitfulness for your glory

Chapter 10

HEART OF SACRIFICE

"Gather My saints together to me, those who have made a covenant with me by sacrifice." Psalms 50:5

Sacrifice is when you give up something you will like to keep, or when you let go of something you wish to hold onto dearly. To make sacrifice is not easy, but sacrifice in itself makes life easy. Sacrifice is giving in pain, in order to gain.

Sacrifice brings satisfaction! It truly takes sacrifice to be satisfied. Until you are willing to pay the price of sacrifice, you are not ready to enjoy the benefits that come with sacrifice. Indeed, your sacrifice to God is what draws God's attention to you. It is an attitude that shows to God that you are willing to give to Him all you have, even when it will cost you so much.

You must learn to continually live a sacrificial life, without holding unto anything more tightly than you should. A heart of sacrifice will be willing to give God anything and everything.

God accepts every offering that comes from a sacrificial heart. Therefore, let your giving, worship, and praise to God be out of a spirit of sacrifice. Interestingly, David was called a man after God's heart because of his life of sacrifice. Also, God blessed Abraham because of his willingness to sacrifice his only son, Isaac, which turned out to be a test from God.

Sacrifice is not about how much you give up, but how costly it is for you to give away that which you are giving. The corrupt human nature is fond of pleasure, but the demand of God is a life of sacrifice. A life which reckons God's gift and rewards as more precious to be received and kept, than the pleasures of the flesh and the world.

In **Luke 9:23-24**, Jesus declares the kind of life a believer in Him must live to experience His fullness. He said:

> *"...if any man will come after me, let him deny himself, and take up his cross daily, and follow me. For whosoever will save his life shall lose it: but whosoever will lose his life for my sake, the same shall save it."*

The way to save your life is to give it away to God for his purpose. The way to protect your relationship is to let it be unto the glory of God, and not unto lust and sexual immorality. The way to save your time is to invest it in worthwhile affairs. The way to secure your future is to invest your today in the things of God and things of eternal values. You don't make more money by hoarding it; you invest it. You have to live a sacrificial life to live fully in this world.

A life of sacrifice is a life that has more in heaven than here on earth. It is a life that knows how to convert earthly treasures, privileges, and opportunities to their eternal equivalents. You must be ready to let go of anything that matters to you here on earth, in order to experience the treasures that come through the sacrifice of Jesus Christ.

Sacrifice is vital to unlocking secret doors in the spirit realm. Jesus commands you:

> ***"Ask, and it shall be given you; seek, and ye shall find; knock, and it shall be opened unto you…" Matthew 7:7***

There are things you will never experience in your life by mere asking, but you will obtain them by sacrifice. Sacrifice is the highest level of prayer that you can ever say to God. Words cannot contain what a sacrifice carries. Hannah, the wife of Elkanah has been going to Shiloh to pray, and to ask for a child, until the day she turned her request to a sacrificial request. She said to the Lord, if you give me a man child, I will give him back to you to serve you. This wasn't an easy thing to do, you know, as this is a child that for years she had trusted God for, and now the child came and she was giving him to God. That's a sacrifice! It was the heart of sacrifice that opened her womb for the boy Samuel to come forth.

(1 Samuel 1:10-19)

Jesus obtained a more excellent name than all the angels (Hebrews 1:4) and all creatures in heaven and on earth and in hell. How? He gave the greatest sacrifice. Only men of sacrifices rule anywhere, anytime. You rise according to the level of the sacrifices you make in life. You can't be different from others if you won't live a different life. Even among believers in Christ, there are differences in glory; because glory goes in the way of sacrifice.

Until you begin to see the demand of God to live a sacrificial life as a call unto glory, you will not rise. No demand of God is designed to harm you or destroy you; they are secret paths to glory, if obeyed.

You need to grow in knowledge, understanding and wisdom of scriptural giving. When you give liberally and cheerfully it makes giving great and attracts the overflowing blessings of God, to the extent that God's grace will abound toward you; that you will always have sufficient in all things. You do not need to wait to have large money or perfect talent before you give. Jesus watched when the people were giving in the temple. The rich, the poor but he was attracted to the Widow who gave wholeheartedly everything she had. The Lord expects us to be a giver as He is ready to bless us all and reward richly on earth and in heaven when we give according to the scripture. God is a giver and he expects those who will relate with Him to have the same spirit of giving. Isaac knew this principle even as he walked with God and he received back in abundant.

Genesis 26:12-13,

> *"Then Isaac sowed in that land, and received in the same year an hundredfold: and the Lord blessed him. And the man waxed great, and went forward, and grew until he became very great. ``*

Again, your sacrifice is vital to initiate a covenant with God. In **Psalms 50:5,**

> *Gather my saints together unto me, those that have made a covenant with me by sacrifice.*

God summoned to Himself, men who have made a covenant with Him by sacrifice. Your sacrifice can initiate an agreement between God and you, which can extend even to generations after you. Some children are enjoying today, simply because of the covenant God made with their fathers, which was initiated by their sacrificial lives. The sacrifice offered by Abraham initiated a covenant with God, that we all enjoy in Christ today. Also, Noah initiated a covenant with God by the sacrifice he offered after the flood (Genesis 8:20-9:17), and that covenant includes the whole earth- the covenant of the rainbow. Sacrifice can also terminate strongholds and battles of life. See the story of the king of Moab, during a fierce battle against the children of Israel- God's own people.

> ***When the king of Moab saw that the battle was too fierce for him, he took with him 700 men who drew swords, to break through to the king of Edom; but they could not. Then he took his oldest son who was to reign in his place, and offered him as a burnt offering on the wall. And there came great wrath against Israel, and they departed from him and returned to their own land. 2 Kings 3:26-27***

God responds to sacrifices! Your sacrifice is a voice that cries out for attention in the presence of God. At any level, your sacrifice speaks. The greater it is, the louder it sounds in heaven. If you have found yourself in situations that seemed indomitable, you can win by sacrifice.

Your sacrifice is a secret invitation to the host of heaven. It is secret because it is a communication between your heart and the Council in heaven.

Now, you must understand that there is no more excellent sacrifice than that which Jesus had offered. And upon the basis of his sacrifice is everything you can obtain in God possible. Your sacrifice has nothing to do with what Jesus has finished in His sacrifice. The grace of God is offered to humankind because Christ paid the price once and forever. However, you experience what God offers more in-depth, and at higher levels, by living a life of sacrifice. The question for you now, is: what are you willing to sacrifice for God? Remember, nothing can be too much to sacrifice for this awesome God.

THINGS TO DO:

Remember:

- Holding tight to what you have without giving leads to poverty - Proverb 11:24
- Giving is a language of love
- Giving to God shows your love to Him
- It is only God who empowered me to have the wealth
- The hands that give gathers
- God is a giver - John 3:16

Prayer Points:

- Lord endow me with the spirit of giving
- Father make me a giver in all areas of my life
- I will not fail to give my tithe, my offering and to those who are in need as you bless me in Jesus' name.

CONCLUSION

In conclusion, God has never asked you to give anything He has not given first. If he asked you to do anything for His sake, He has undoubtedly done much more for your sake. If He demands faithfulness from you, he is faithful. If he demands holiness from you, he is holy. If He requires love from you, he is love, and he loves you. If He demands a life of sacrifice from you, he has ever been sacrificing for you.

God has not required anything from you that he has not given Himself. All He wants to do with your life, and with all his demands, is to shape your life after Him. God wants you to obtain results on earth that are after His kind. All of God's requirements is to make you and not to destroy you. God's expectation from you is to enable you to enjoy a good relationship with Him and with people around you. Being able to meet God's expectation raises you, and gives you a direction in life.

Overall, in the process of knowing you measure or stand on what God's expect from you, you do not have to compare yourself with everybody else. If you do, you will always look fine and not see any imperfection or the other way round condemned yourself as not measure to standard and get discouraged. Romans 12:2. Instead, you are to compare yourself to Jesus Christ and your character should be Christlike. The word of God admonishes us to work toward perfection not as anyone else but like our Father in heaven:

> ***Be ye therefore perfect, even as your Father which is in heaven is perfect. Matthew 5:48***

> ***But we all, with open face beholding as in a glass the glory of the Lord, are changed into the same image from glory to glory, even as by the Spirit of the Lord. 2Corinthians 3:18***

Someone asked Jesus, that of all the commandments, which was the greatest. In reply Jesus replied:

> ***Jesus said unto him, Thou shall love the Lord thy God with all thy heart, and with all thy heart, and with all thy soul, and with all thy mind. This is the first and great commandment. And the second is the like unto it. Thou shalt love thy neighbour as thyself-Matthew 22:37-39***

In excess, everything God expect from us boiled down to one word- LOVE.

Finally, the core of God's expectation is for us to be saved and to make heaven.

> ***For God so loved the world, that He gave His only begotten Son, that whosoever beliveth in Him should not perish, but have everlasting life. John 3:16***

You cannot afford to miss that. God bless you.

www.ingramcontent.com/pod-product-compliance
Lightning Source LLC
Chambersburg PA
CBHW071212130726

47998CB00002B/712